SUBWAY SWINGER

poems and drawings by
VIRGINIA SCHONBORG

William Morrow and Company
New York

SUBWAY SWINGER (COMING)

Subway swinger,
Cowboy from Brooklyn,
Astronaut from the Bronx,
Tunneling through Manhattan rock,
Watch the track ahead
As you sway on your horse,
As you swing through space.
The green lights say, "Go."
You're getting somewhere, boy!

PARK SPRING

Balloons bloom
In the tall trees;
Frisbies are flying
Across the park;
Skates screech
On the pavement.
Now the air is tender,
The ground is muddy,
The kids are yelling.
City spring
Comes swiftly.
Everyone is out
To catch it!

BIRTHDAY BIKE

There it stood,
Sleek, shining, red.
I heard the voice
"Ride it in the parking lot,
Don't ride it in the street!"
Down the stairway
I bumped and bumpled
My new bike.
The wind sang in my ears;
My muscles felt good.
I streaked across the parking lot.
It rode smooth as silk
And steered on the curves
Like a racer.
Did I ride it
In the parking lot?
You bet!
Will I ride it
In the street?
Soon.

IN THEIR CAGES

They live there
Prowling by day
And night,
Padding, turning.
The big cats
Hardly ever
Look at me.
In their cages
The hippos
Snuffle into the water,
Big-eyed and sad.
They look past me.
The monkeys swing
And scratch,
Swing
And scratch.
They look at me.
Their toy hands know
I'm good for a peanut.
The big apes

Turn their backs to me
In their cages.
I know how they feel
In the zoo,
In their cages,
In the city.

CITY RAIN

When you walk
At night
In the rain,
And the city lights come on,
You walk in pools
Of scarlet,
Of purple.
You walk in pools
Of shimmering green.
The colors mix
In the palette
At your feet,
As you walk
By night
In the city rain.

SOOTY BROTHER

Sooty brother,
I know your bright cousin
In other greener places.
City sparrow,
House sparrow,
Hoodlum,
They call you.
You're quick
Like me,
And you go after
What you want.
You're a tough boy
In the city.
You build your nest
In the dingy tree.
You build
With old twigs
And dirty string.
You take care of your young.
City sparrow.

TRAFFIC

The heavy sound of it,
It's always there,
Like a wind
Roaring toward me.
The lighter sounds,
The bleats, the honks, the shrieks
Of the sheeplike cars
Are in the middle.
Except—
Except in the dry light
Of early day.
I wake up
At four A.M.
Nothing.
No wind,
Only heels in the street,
Sharp echoes.
A voice murmuring,
The thin song
Of early sparrows.

In an hour or two
The wind will rise again.
The heavy sound of the city,
It's almost always there.

STICKBALL

The broomstick bat
Is good.
You've got to be fast,
You've got to dodge.
Stickball's a tough game
In the city.
The ball ricochets
From fender to hood
To stoop—you've got it!
You've got to be fast,
You've got to dodge
In the city.

CONEY

There's hot corn
And franks.
There's the boardwalk
With lots of games,
With chances
To win or lose.
There's the sun.
Underneath the boardwalk
It's cool,
And the sand is salty.
The beach is
Like a fruitstand of people,
Big and little,
Red and white,
Brown and yellow.
There's the sea
With high green waves.
And after,
There's hot corn
And franks.

HOT

Heat
In the street
Is a heavy heat,
A slow heat.
It doesn't move.
We sit on the stoop.
We play cards.
They're gummy
With the heat.
"Play your card,
You cheat!"
When I close my eyes,
It's red
Behind my eyelids.
Hey!
The hydrant's open!
Take the cards.
C'mon,
Beat the heat!

HYDRANT

In the steaming street
The hydrant, wide-open,
Rushed,
Churned,
Sprayed,
Ran a wide river in the gutter.
The boy's brown fingers
Forced the flood
To green and blue
And gold.
Through his fingers
A rainbow grew.
The kids screamed
And danced
In and out,
In and out.
Remember how wet it was?
Remember how cold?

IN MY NEIGHBORHOOD

In my neighborhood
It's nice.
We meet
At the candy store
And laugh and buy
One Pepsi for three.
It's O.K. with Mr. Santos.
In my neighborhood
There's a playground
With swings,
And a new climbing thing
Like a tree house.
It's great to climb up high.
In my neighborhood
There are people I know
On the block.
I know the lady
Who sells the cloth
My mother buys:
Red and yellow,

Shining flowered cloth.
I know the pickle man.
Sometimes—
He gives me a pickle!
In my neighborhood
It's very nice.

SIDEWALK SUPER

There are holes
In the fence
For people
With long legs,
With short legs.
I look through
Way down below.
I see a red crane working,
I see orange hats shining,
I see a biting yellow steam shovel,
Gnawing out the earth and rock.
Every day I come
And look through
Way down below.
I see it change
From a shadowy hole
To a steel scaffold,
To a shining building.
I'm a sidewalk super!

LADY COP

The lady cop
Steers the traffic.
She makes it stop
For us to cross from school,
Just like a regular cop.
All in blue, with a cap.
But when my brother
Had a bloody nose,
She had a Kleenex in her pocket.
She's O.K.

A RUMBLE

They roar
Out of the river tunnels
Into the streaming streets,
As strong
As a pride of lions,
As long
As a gaggle of geese.
A rumble of trucks
Streaks through the city.
I'd like to drive one
Towering over taxis,
Diesels smoking!
I'd like to drive one,
Cars pulling over,
Cops waving!
I'd like to streak
Through the city
Part of
A rumble of trucks.

SONG OF SHIPS

The air was damp,
And it smelled of the sea
On that dark night,
Walking home.
I heard a sea gull
Crying,
And, distant,
The sad song of ships
Creeping through the fog.
I thought,
These hard pavements
Really reach to the sea.

"NO PETS ALLOWED"

In my project
It says,
"No pets allowed."
But in school
I'm the rabbit keeper.
His name is Jumper.
Across the room
His rabbit feet
Jump him along to me,
His soft feet sliding.
His nose plays with my shoes.
I pat his furry
Black-and-white body.
I'm his keeper.
Someday
I'll build a project,
And there will be
"Pets allowed."

MIRA! MIRA!

Mira! Mira!
Mirror on the wall
Who's the fairest of them all?
Rosa?
Maria?
Angela?
Or is it José
In his white shirt
For Assembly day?

MESSAGES

In Dayglo red
On the dark subway walls
Messages meet me.
At 53rd and Lexington
"Margie, drop dead."
"The Cavaliers,
The Lords were here."
On the walls of the school,
"José loves Inez."
"John loves Mary."
Even on buses
There are messages,
"Feed a squirrel."
Everybody is sending messages
To the world.

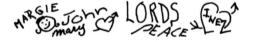

CONSTRUCTION

Wham!
Comes the wrecking ball.
Wham!
And the bricks fly.
I see where people lived
In rooms with pale blue walls,
Pale green, pale rose.
Wham!
A whole wall crumples,
Sinks into red dust.
I see where people have lived.
Wham!
I see old tables
And a bed.
Where did they go,
The people who lived
In the rooms with pale blue walls,
Pale green, pale rose?

CROWDS

Crowds pushing
Into the subway
Scare me.
(Maybe I'll grow out of it.)
Crowds rushing
At the traffic light
Make me wonder.
Crowds
Passing
Dashing
Across the honking streets
Carry me along.
Crowds that stand
In
Long
Lines
Forever
For a ticket,
For a movie,
I don't dig.

Crowds
Slicking
Up and down escalators,
Crowds
Popping out of elevators
Don't turn me on.
(Maybe I'll grow out of it.)

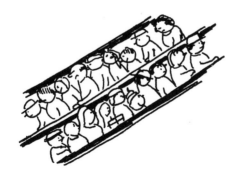

RESCUE

Bony cat,
Scrabbling along
In the sleet,
You need a child
To warm you.
I'll take you, cat,
Where it's dry,
And there's a can of milk.
I'll feed you, Bony.
We'll be friends.
No more hiding
Under cars,
No more crying.
We'll be friends,
Bony cat,
Scrabbling along
In the sleet.

SKATER

The sun is silver
In November,
Cold on your fingers
As you fumble your skate key.
But the air is clear and windy
As you fling around the corner,
Skirt ballooning,
Hair streaking,
Eyes watering!

CHANGE

Snow the first,
Snow the beautiful,
Falling, darting, rising.
Small stars
Playing in the white world.
Everything changes.
Tarred roofs
Into white fields;
Water towers
Into farmers' silos.
Smoke blooms and sways,
A charcoal flower
Against the sky.
Snow changes me,
Snow changes you,
City child
To
Country child.

MERRY CHRISTMAS

The bird dashes
To the alien tree,
The broken glitter of Christmas
Silver-shot and shattered
In the gutter.
Children's eyes
No longer gleam
In the tree's light.
But what a green feast
Of pine and needle
For the murky city sparrow!

SUBWAY SWINGER (GOING)

Subway swinger,
Cowboy from Brooklyn,
Astronaut from the Bronx,
Tunneling through Manhattan rock,
Watch the track ahead
As you sway on your horse,
As you swing through space.
The green lights say, "Go."
Go,
Travel,
Think,
Dream in the city.
You're getting somewhere, boy!